JUST A
COG IN THE
WHEEL

JUST A COG IN THE WHEEL

by Joseph Farris

BOB ADAMS, INC.
HOLBROOK, MASSACHUSETTS

ISBN: 1-55850-902-X

10 9 8 7 6 5 4 3 2 1

Published by Bob Adams, Inc., 260 Center Street,
Holbrook, MA 02343.

Printed in the United States of America.

Portions of this book appeared previously in: The
American Bar Association Press; American Management
Association publications; American Psychological
Association publications; Barron's; Changing Times;
Crain's New York Business; Dartnell Corporation
publications; Goodlife; The Harvard Business Review;
High Tech Marketing; Medical Economics; New Woman;
The New York Daily News; The New Yorker.
Illustrations reprinted by permission.

To Christine and Erik Andersen.

"I realize that this might be carping but I never did live long enough to enjoy my I.R.A. account."

"Where's everybody?"

"He has an MBA from Wharton."

"Looks like the gods are angry."

"Miss Raleigh, I'm studying megatrends.
Bring me some megavitamins."

*"What do you mean, I have an ulcer?
I give ulcers, I don't get them!"*

"I'm not asking for a raise, Mr. Betenheeler, but would it be possible for you to treat me as a human being?"

*"You are a credit to the human race, Yardsley.
Unfortunately, you're a liability to this firm."*

"Clear your desk. You're fired!"

"We're just beginning."

"It was his last wish."

*"How can a man jump out of a window
if the damned window can't be opened!"*

"Miss Wayson, find out who put this computer on my desk and tell them to get it the hell out of here!"

"Which should I be worrying about? The wholesale price index,
the consumer price index, or the industrial price index?"

"Look...people are basically honest and decent. Why don't we scrap the tax laws completely and have the people pay whatever they think is fair?"

"What else do you have going for you besides being aggressive?"

*"It so happens, I think of myself as a C.E.O. first,
then as a human being!"*

"Since we think alike, why don't I put all my assets in a blind trust managed by you and you put all your assets in a blind trust managed by me?"

"Perk up. Just think of all that interest piling up at more than 5% per annum."

"All those in favor of making more loans, raise you hands."

"Before we start, has every one shed their moral baggage?"

"I took your advice and told him either I get a promotion or I quit!"

"My problem is that I'm number one in my field and I have no place to go but down."

*"Kellerman, eh? I didn't recognize the face,
but the voice-over was familiar."*

"It's me, Paul Newman, speeding by in my racing car."

"I feel more secure surrounded by things."

"You're all a bunch of clowns. You're all fired."

*"I highly recommend this painting
if you're interested in art as an investment."*

"Gentlemen, and Ladies, today we're going to get down to nuts and bolts..."

Whistle blowers

"A representative from Merrill Lynch to see you."

"There goes J.B., still unflappable."

"I'll be late for dinner, Dear.
I'm up to my neck in paperwork."

"I knew insects wouldn't take over the world...numbers will!"

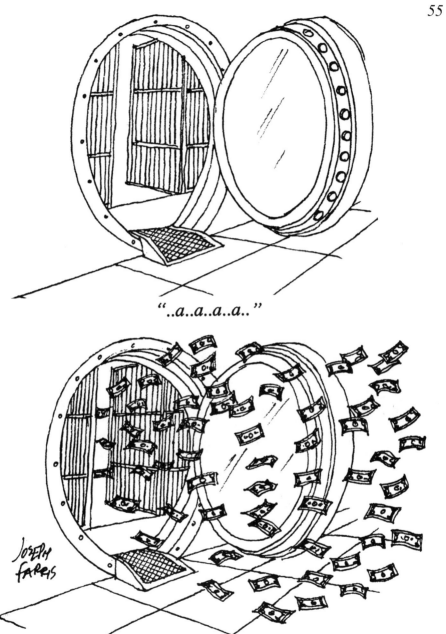

"..a..a..a..a.."

"..choo!!"

"*Fersteimer believes in strictly minding his own business.*"

*"Let's play business. I'll be the Chairman of the Board and
you'll work for me and laugh whenever I tell a joke."*

"When the poor dear retired, he found that he missed his little cubicle."

"Buy...sell...buy...sell...buy..."

"The only exercise I believe in is the exercise of power."

"This should be good. He just won the lottery!"

"Enough small talk. It's time for big talk."

"It's true. There <u>was</u> a coup!"

"Oh, Cynthia, I must tell you. I just found the cutest little mutual fund..."

"Need I remind you who is boss here?"

"You say he left the office hours ago?"

"It's all right. I'm just a little behind."

*"I've never had to butter up the boss.
I've always <u>been</u> the boss."*

*"I'm feeling absolutely marvelous.
I think I'll acquire another company."*

"Which track is the gravy train on?"

"What do you have for someone on the way down?"

"But I do have fun. I have lots of fun. I have lots of fun making lots of money."

"Big shots deserve big offices."

"Sir, I need stroking."

"A lackluster style got me where I am, and a lackluster style is going to keep me here."

"It was a power struggle but I won!"

"I've stopped going out at night. Too dangerous."

"Morston, why aren't you taking your worries home with you?"

"I remember when the spotlight was on <u>me</u>!"

"Call the office. I'm starting my vacation today."

"Meet the Nobel Laureates of my sales departments."

"Need I tell you the name of the game?"

"My philosophy has always been, sell advice, don't follow it."

"Have you met my vice-presidents?"

"Do you know who you're addressing?"

"When I make a mistake it's a beaut!"

"My Christmas bonus."

"Oh no...not here too!"

"You're a little <u>too</u> small."

"Don't just stand there doing nothing! Sell yourself a suit!"

"I did get a raise. Could that be it?"

"It's creative as hell! Now that you've got that out of your system, give me a campaign that will sell."

"Someday, daughter, this will all be yours."

"It all began when they exchanged pleasantries."

"*Pay no attention to him. He's just a disgruntled former employee.*"

*"You've got plenty of time for a little prayer
before you get to him."*

"We're very tight on space right now but we'll have you in an office as soon as we can. Meanwhile..."

"No, not <u>your</u> Uncle Sam. <u>The</u> Uncle Sam!"

"I'm curious. What part of New York City are we in?"

"Don't bother me with facts. Tell me what I want to hear."

"I brought in a big order and my boss gave me a feather for my cap."

"I sure wish there was a formula for picking the right mutual fund!"

"It's my spare tire. Why do you ask?"

"Looks like Kryson is no longer in the inner circle."

"The boss is in a good mood if you want to ask for a raise."

"I don't know how they dispose of our toxic wastes and I don't want to know."

"Our most valued employees."

"I think it's a hostile takeover!"

"I usually fly first class but it doesn't compare to this super-duper, extra special, state-of-the-art, WOW class."

"We're a bit tight on space."

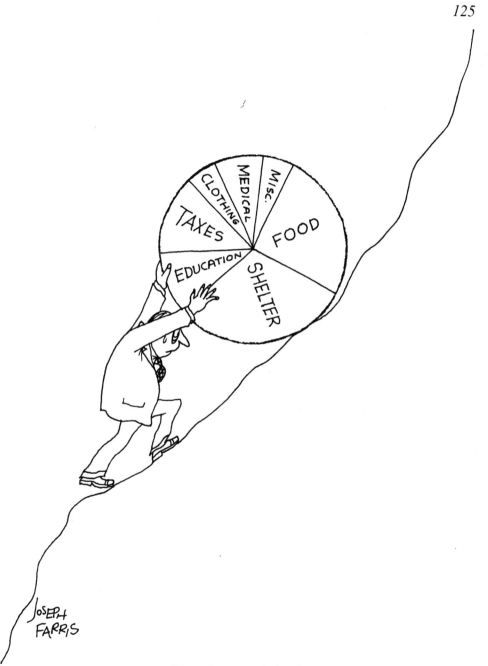

Sisyphus revisited

"Let's play house. You do the cooking and cleaning
and I'll go to the office."

"I gave at the office!"

"Get the hell back in here!
Are you trying to give our firm a bad name?"

"I like your attitude, Brigley."

"Miss Wyeth, would you merge your corporation with mine?"

"Miss Hale, it's my birthday. Tell the employees
they have an extra five minutes for their coffee break."

*"I'm moving up to be Chairperson-of-the-Board.
One of you will be President."*

"Now, what's your complaint?"

"Don't have me beeped. I'll have you beeped."

"Pardon me. Can you tell me where 9 West 57th is?"

"He runs a marvelously disciplined corporation."

"Marjorie, look! Free prospectuses!"

"Has deregulation hurt you?"

"No one showed up. Everyone is working."

"By golly, I'm going to sink another hundred thousand into IBM!"

"I give you the city, Fuller. Go out there and sell!"

"We're a very, very old firm."

"Put it in writing."

"There's quite a power struggle going on."

"Guess who made a bushel today?"

"I had a nightmare last night. I dreamed I was let go by the public sector and not wanted by the private sector."

"*My philosophy is to sit down
and the hell with being counted!*"

"I understand he's here on a business trip."

*"My mother sent down some chicken soup
to see if that will help."*

*I say we adjourn. We've already mortgaged
all the foreseeable future."*

"I want three one-cent stamps, two twos, one three, three fours, two fives, one six, one seven, two eights, one nine, one ten, two elevens, one thirteen, one fifteen, two eighteens..."

"I'm not running for reelection.
I already have enough material for my book."

"O.K. We're Japanese art buyers. Do we buy it?"

"*I have diplomatic immunity!*"

"Majorie, I wasn't kicked upstairs after all!"

"Do you mind if I take the rest of my session to get your input on investor psychology?"

WHAT IS POSSIBLE   WHAT IS PROBABLE

"I don't know where the bad guys are. I'm a good guy."

The Four Sides of W. Amherst Faunton

boss   *husband*   *father*   *friend*

Joseph Farris is a cartoonist for the *New Yorker*, where many of the cartoons in this, his first book, have previously appeared — as well as in such other magazines as *Barron's*, and *The Harvard Business Review*.